Country Needleworks

Country Needleworks

Complete patterns and instructions
for over 28 projects
inspired by American folk designs

Stephen & Carol Huber

Artwork by Chesca Sheldon
Stitching by Betty Voulgaris, Martha Neal
and Jacqui Clarkson
Photos by Stephen Huber

S. & C. Huber, American Classics
East Lyme, Ct.

Chesca Sheldon at work.

First Edition

Other Publications by Stephen & Carol Huber: Countryknits, Countryknits For Kids, Countryknits II.

CONTENTS

INTRODUCTION

"Why don't you do a book for needlepoint and cross-stitch with these wonderful designs?"

This is the question we have heard over and over from shop owners nationwide while doing needlework shows across the country. So here it is — some of our "Country" knitting patterns converted for cross-stitch and needlepoint.

This project has opened a whole new area to us and we have had a great time designing and thinking through this book. We hope this will be an inspiring guide, one that will give you lots of ideas, with graphs that can be used in a multitude of ways.

We have included some basic notes on needlepoint and counted cross-stitch, illustrations showing the stitches we have used, blocking and finishing instructions, complete directions and graphs for 28 projects, and a chart showing the name of the pattern and ideas for its use. We think this latter will be of great value for triggering your imagination and then working up a variety of projects. With an emphasis on Americana, many of our patterns blend together and more than one can be used in a project. Experiment, sketch, and come up with your own configuration of our graphs. Remember, our graphs can be used for needlepoint *or* counted cross-stitch.

At the end of the book we have included a few names and addresses for some of the various supplies we have used throughout our projects. You will find them helpful if your local shop does not carry the items you need.

On the home front (for those of you who have all our books and read the introductions), our daughter, Chesca, has just graduated from college and plans to pursue a career in the graphic arts. We're hoping she will have a little time to "moonlight" and continue to assist us with our new designs and books. The barn is overflowing with books, packing boxes, yarn, bags, kit supplies, etc. Our plans to build a new barn on the property here were set aside as a nearby 18th-century center chimney house with barns will soon become available and we will be able to move the business to that location and keep our 17th-century farm as a

home. In the meantime, Steve pitched the old camping tent in the yard and we have it chuck full of yarn. Ochipee the llama (and my engagement present from Steve) died. He was getting old, but my theory is he developed Lyme Disease. We are off to England this month to work with our knitters and to design for the upcoming book "Countryknits III." We are looking forward to a few weeks of uninterrupted design time and the glorious English countryside.

But, back to this book, and the marvelous time we have had working on it. It has been great, only because we have worked with so many helpful and talented people. Our stitching, and many ideas, came from three wonderful ladies we met at one of the National Needlework Shows. Betty Voulgaris, Martha Neal and Jacqui Clarkson were all invaluable to this production. They meticulously did the stitching, revised graphs, and always met their deadlines. A great big thank you!

We are also most appreciative of the many companies that contributed supplies or finishing work. American Crewel and Canvas, for canvas and yarn; A. Zeller Belt Co., for finishing and donating supplies for the belts; Cottage Needlepoint, for their wonderful array of totes; Johnson Creative Crafts, for yarns and other supplies; K's Creations, for their marvelous frames; and Sudbury House for their generous donation of beautiful boxes, trays, coasters, benches, clocks and more. Thank you all!

We would also like to thank our printer, Harvey Hoechstetter, and his assistant, Alice Wahl, for their advice, personal interest and professional help with this, our first book to be published by *us*.

And, last but not least, a very special thank you to Chesca, our daughter, who always comes to the aid of her parents in a talented and loving way. Her easy-to-follow graphs make needlework a joy!

Well, there you have it. We hope you love it and we would like very much to hear from you, the needleworkers, with pictures, letters or calls. Let us know your thoughts. Happy needleworking!

NEEDLEPOINT NOTES

We thought a few very basic notes on Needlepoint would be a helpful addition to this book. This is not a "how-to" book so our pointers are not in detail — just a refresher.

Allow 1½″ of canvas on all sides of design — needed for blocking and finishing.

Prepare canvas by covering edges with masking tape or seam binding.

Mark center by folding in half and in half again. Mark top and bottom center also.

Stitch tension should be even. Pulling too tight will leave canvas showing. Too loose and piece will look bumpy.

Left-handed needleworkers should turn the stitch diagram upside-down and follow the numbers.

When beginning new thread, bring the needle up through the canvas and leave a 1½″ tail. Hold the tail in the direction you are stitching and cover the tail with the backs of the stitches four or five times. Later, trim off ends.

When ending a yarn, slide needle through four or five stitches and clip close to work.

Frames and embroidery hoops are especially important because they help eliminate stretching. We have used lap frames from K's Creations (see listing at back of book) exclusively and are extremely pleased with their products.

Our charts are charted as Berlin Work charts. The squares represent one stitch.

Paternayan yarn comes with three strands of 3-ply each to make a unit. In this book, we will refer to 2-ply as being two threads each of 3-ply. In other words, remove one of the 3-ply strands. The yarn comes twisted, so make sure to untwist each strand before starting and put them back together. This permits fuller coverage of the canvas.

Notes

TWEEDING

A great technique for creating a color, toning down one too bright or lightening up one too dark, is to "tweed." This is a method of combining two or more colors to make a new one. It is an easy and exciting way to work with color. It can be done with cotton, silk or wool with great results.

Cotton yarn gives the most versatility as you can use 6-ply cotton floss on 18-mesh canvas. Wool works well, but because it is heavier, only two or three colors may be used.

To look at your new color before you create and stitch with it, twist the colors together without separating them. This will give an idea of what the final results will be when stitched. Remember when stitching that dark colors show up intricate stitches less than light colors. So, if you want your stitches to be most prominent, don't go too dark.

Tweeding works well in needlepoint for shading, changing from one color to another, and for interest when doing large areas. It is a technique that is fun to use, and sometimes a great way to use up oddments of yarn.

Notes

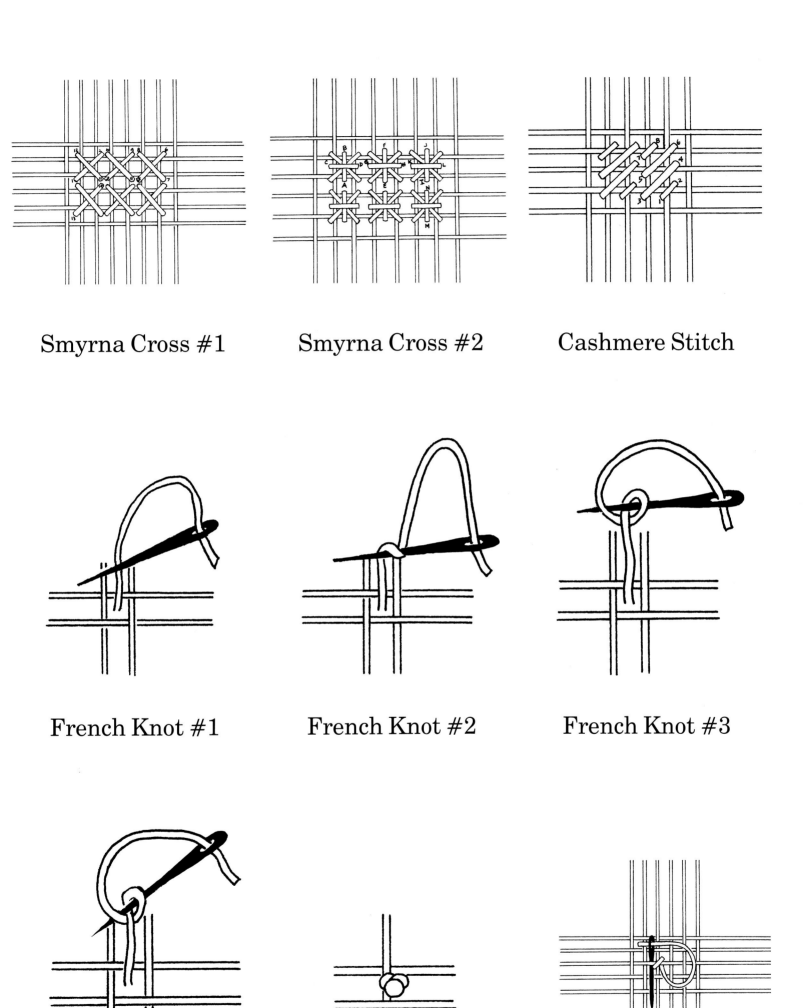

Smyrna Cross #1 Smyrna Cross #2 Cashmere Stitch

French Knot #1 French Knot #2 French Knot #3

French Knot #4 French Knot #5 Greek Stitch #1

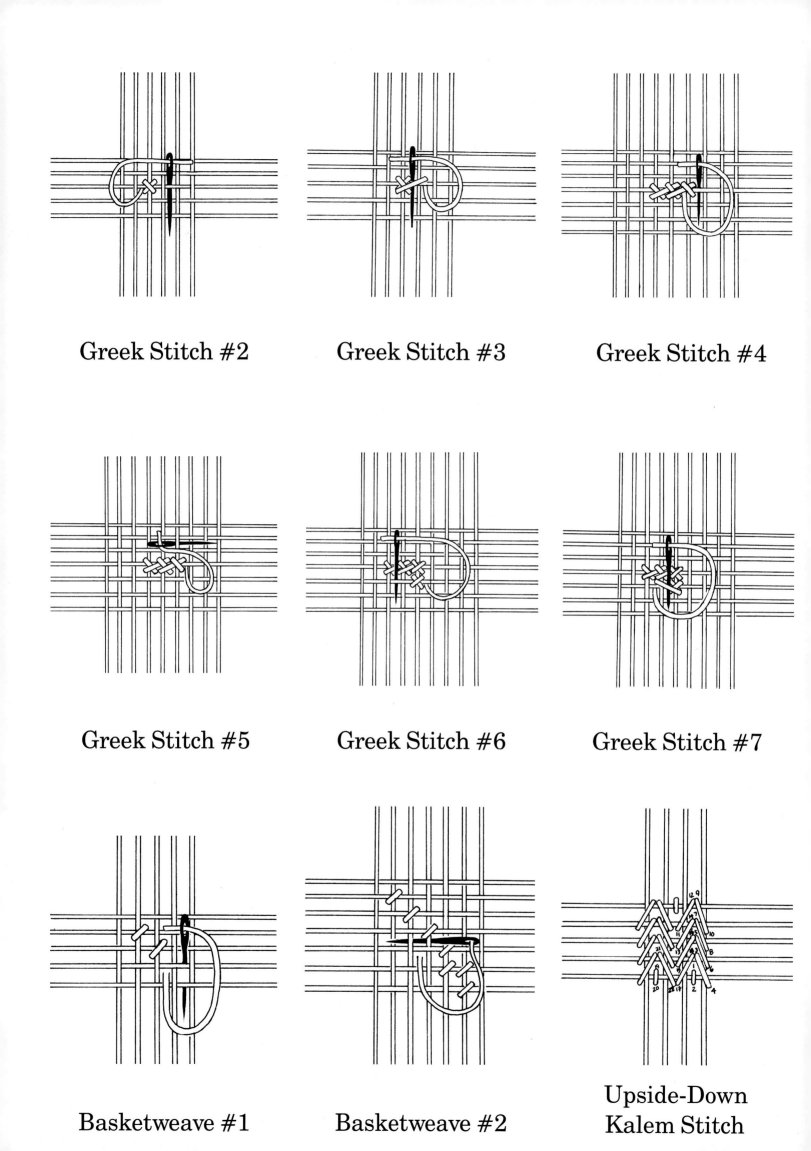

Greek Stitch #2

Greek Stitch #3

Greek Stitch #4

Greek Stitch #5

Greek Stitch #6

Greek Stitch #7

Basketweave #1

Basketweave #2

Upside-Down
Kalem Stitch

COUNTED CROSS-STITCH NOTES

Allow 3″ of extra fabric on all sides of design, especially large pieces such as samplers. This will allow plenty of room for finishing and framing.

Prepare the fabric by taping or zigzagging around all edges to keep from fraying.

Find the center of the fabric by folding in half and in half again, following the straight of the fabric. Mark by basting with a contrasting thread along the folds.

Use an embroidery hoop to keep the fabric taut. Right-handed, put the screw at 10 o'clock, left-handed, at 2 o'clock. This keeps the thread from tangling. Small pieces do not require the use of a frame. K's Creations carry excellent frames (see listing at back of book).

Do not knot thread; they show through and leave bumps. When starting a new thread, leave a 1½″ tail and work the first four or five stitches over it on the back side.

When ending a thread, carry it through four or five stitches on the back side.

Do not carry thread from one motif to the next, even if they are the same color. It shows through.

Work in a stab-stick method. Put the needle completely through the hole before you bring it up through the next.

For best results, work first half the stitches across and then half stitches back.

Use a blunt tapestry needle. Do not leave it in design when not stitching. Use size 24 needle for Aida 11 and 14, size 26 needle for Aida 18 and 22.

Wash project before framing or finishing. Use a mild soap and cold water. Rinse thoroughly and roll in a towel to pat dry. Press on wrong side of fabric.

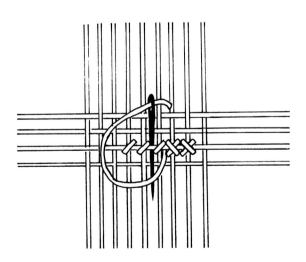

Cross Stitch

CANDLEWICKING

Candlewicking is a very old form of embroidery, using actual candle wick on a cotton background. It was very popular in the late 18th and early-to-mid-19th century. Used primarily for bed covers, pillow shams and table runners, this was a very effective and inexpensive method of making a decorative textile. Much quicker than quilting and piecing, or spinning and weaving, these white-on-white textiles were usually very original in design and often contained personal emblems, dates, objects and initials. Enjoying a recent surge in popularity, Candlewicking is easy to work, only requires two stitches, and is done with candle-wick cotton yarn on a muslin or other cotton background.

Notes

BELTS

Hints for making Needlepoint Belts:

1. Determine belt size (true waist): Measure old belt of person from inside edge of belt buckle to hole where belt is fastened.

2. Determine overall needlepoint length (ONL): Subtract 4″ from belt size.

3. Determine maximum design length: Subtract 6″ from ONL found in step 2.

4. Center design (length of design can be less than maximum design length found in step 3.

5. For any width belt, add two extra rows of background needlepoint along each edge. (These rows will be folded under when belt is mounted.)

6. Leave extra scrim around all edges of needlepoint.

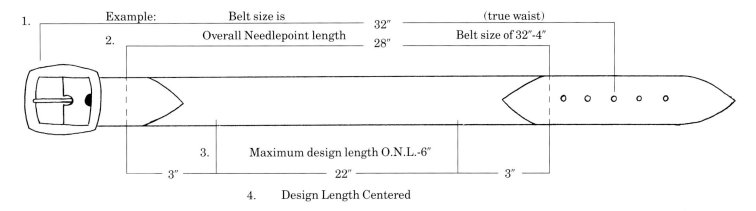

Belts can be made by having your local needlepoint shop contact A. Zeller Belt Manufacturing Company (see suppliers). Or you can contact Needlepoint Country (see suppliers).

Notes

BLOCKING EMBROIDERY WORK

Make sure embroidery work is clean.

Place right-side down on padded surface. Pin into shape so that grain of fabric is straight in both directions.

Using a clean sponge and distilled water, moisten the needlework thoroughly by patting the sponge evenly on the fabric. Do not rub or soak.

Allow to dry 24 hours, remove pins and finish as required.

BLOCKING CANVASWORK

If you have used a frame and your tension is somewhat regular, you probably will not have to block your finished piece. If, however, it is slightly distorted, you can block it using the following simple procedures. We suggest you take extremely distorted pieces to a professional needlepoint shop for their opinion.

Only block clean needlework. If it is soiled, have it professionally dry-cleaned, omitting the pressing or ironing.

Place right-side down on a padded surface, cover with dampened pressing cloth.

Press lightly with iron set at "wool."

While slightly damp, stretch into shape and press again. Pin into shape and allow to dry overnight.

Chart for Additional Projects

Graph	Pillow	Picture	Tote/Handbag	Book Cover	Coasters	Eyeglass Case	Rug	Checkbook Cover	Luggage Straps	Afghan	Placemats	Towels	Apron	Tray	Box	Stool/Chest
Rabbit with Flowers	•	•	•				•			•			•	•		•
Patchwork	•		•	•	•	•	•	•		•	•	•	•	•	•	•
Navajo Railroad	•	•	•				•	•						•		•
Pig-on-a-Rug	•	•	•	•			•			•			•	•		•
Flying Geese	•		•	•	•	•	•	•	•	•	•	•	•	•	•	•
Sampler	•	•	•				•							•		•
Patchwork Star	•		•	•	•	•	•	•		•			•	•	•	•
Watermelon					•	•	•	•			•	•				
Country Goose	•	•	•	•			•			•	•		•	•		•
Indian Blanket	•		•	•	•	•	•	•	•	•	•	•	•	•	•	•
Shaker Tree-of-Life	•	•	•	•										•		•
Log Cabin	•		•	•	•	•	•	•		•			•	•	•	•
Moored Boats	•	•	•	•			•			•			•	•		•
Indiana Fan	•		•	•	•	•	•	•		•				•	•	•
Towne Border	•	•	•	•	•	•	•	•	•	•	•	•	•	•	•	•
Oriental Rug	•		•	•	•	•	•	•	•	•			•	•	•	•
Reindeer and Pine Trees	•	•	•	•			•			•				•		•
Flower and Vine	•		•		•		•			•				•		•
Irish Chain	•		•	•										•	•	•
House Border				•	•	•		•			•	•	•	•	•	
Smutt-the-Cat	•	•	•				•							•	•	•
Heart and Hand	•		•	•			•			•				•		•

Rabbit with Flowers Pillow

A charming pillow with a central rabbit motif surrounded by a field of flowers and a ribbon border. He will adapt to a number of "country-style" projects in a whole array of colors. (Try one with the flowers all different colors.)

MATERIALS: 13 mesh mono canvas, 16″ x 16″, Paternayan wool yarn.

COLORS:
    Rabbit—262 Ecru
            221 Grey
            220 Black
    Background—663 Light Green
    Flowers—953 Strawberry
            661 Dark Green
            727 Soft Yellow
    Border—953 Strawberry
    262 Ecru
    663 Light Green
    661 Dark Green

STITCHES: Rabbit and Flowers Continental, Background Cashmere Stitch. Work with 2-ply.

DIRECTIONS: Find center of canvas and count out to edge of rabbit. Work outline of rabbit and fill in. Start flower off bunny's tail, count up and sideways for distribution. Center of flower is French knot. Work background and border following charts.

NOTES: See sections on *NEEDLEPOINT NOTES, BLOCKING, ADDITIONAL PROJECTS.*

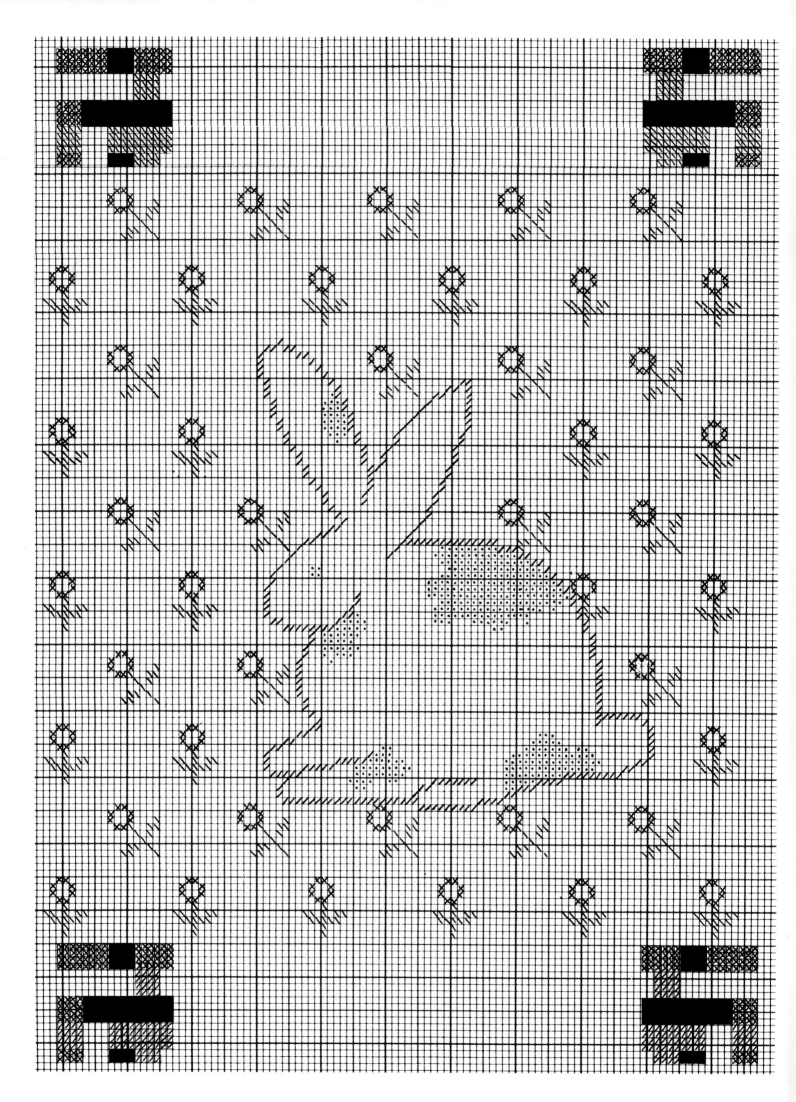

Patchwork Coasters

A medley of quilt designs combine to make this series of coasters. Make them in any combination, all the same, two and two, or all different. Enlarged they are great pillows.

MATERIALS: Fidler's Lite cloth—14 count (Charles Craft), DMC embroidery floss, set of four coasters from Sudbury House.

COLORS: Pot-of-Flowers: Flowers 783 and 221, Squares 317, Leaves 3345, Basket 322 and 310.

Strawberry: Strawberry 350, Leaves 3345, Lines 317, Diamond 783.

Baskets: Baskets 311 and 783, Diamonds 221.

Diamond-with-Flower: Flowers 350, 322 and 783, Lines 221, Leaves 3345.

STITCHES: Counted Cross-Stitch. Work with 2 strands.

DIRECTIONS: Cut fabric on the diagonal to fit coaster insert adding 1″ on each side. Work pattern on straight of fabric. Sew fabric backing on following design shape, use cardboard plus 2-3 Aida threads to get the correct shape. Sew on three sides with machine. Insert cardboard. Turn in top and bottom of fourth side and slip stitch.

NOTES: See sections on *COUNTED CROSS-STITCH, BLOCKING, ADDITIONAL PROJECTS.*

Navajo Railroad Belt

This colorful belt is inspired by a marvelous Navajo blanket woven in the late 19th century. The colors are similar to those of the blanket which commemorates the opening of the railroad in the west. Adapted to a belt, it looks great with country casual and traditional clothing.

MATERIALS: 13 mesh mono canvas, length of belt plus 4 inches and 5-inch width, Paternayan wool yarn.

COLORS:

930 Background
220 Black
262 White Car
663 Green Cars
741 Gold Car
714 Light Yellow
502 Dark Blue
504 Light Blue Cars

STITCHES: Continental for train and arrow. Basketweave for background. Work with 2-ply.

DIRECTIONS: Find center of canvas and work from middle toward ends. Needlepoint on belt will be 1¼″ plus 2 extra rows of background needlepoint along each edge. (These rows will be folded under when belt is mounted.)

NOTES: See sections on *NEEDLEPOINT NOTES, STITCHES, BELTS, BLOCKING, ADDITIONAL PROJECTS.*

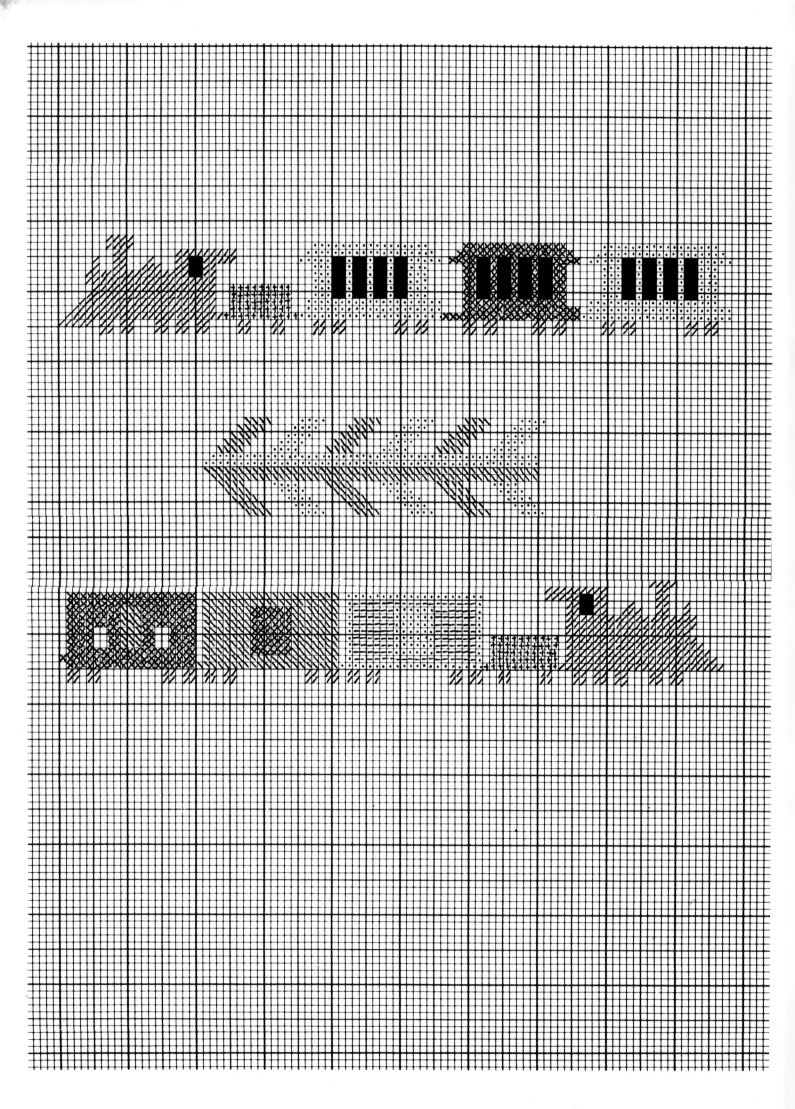

Pig-On-A-Rug Tray

Our pig, a fat little porker, comes from the central motif of a 19th-century hooked rug. He's great fun for a kitchen or picnic "Country"-themed tray.

MATERIALS: Willow Green Aida, cloth, count 14, size 13″ x 13″, DMC embroidery floss, Small Square Tray from Sudbury House.

COLORS: Pig—317 and 224
Rug—99 (varigated)
Flowers—223 and 319
Border—319
Hearts—223
Eye—310 + 1 Blending Filament

STITCHES: Counted Cross-Stitch. Work with 2 strands.

DIRECTIONS: Find center of fabric. Outline pig and work first. Work rug and flowers. Work border. Press and insert into tray.

NOTES: See sections on *COUNTED CROSS-STITCH, BLOCKING, ADDITIONAL PROJECTS.*

Flying Geese Luggage Straps

A popular and colorful pattern, Flying Geese lends itself exceptionally well to luggage straps, bell pulls and a host of other projects. A 19th-century quilt design, it was often made with oddments of leftover fabric. In needlepoint it is a great way to use up yarn left in your work basket. We know you will enjoy the many variations for which this pattern can be used.

MATERIALS: 13 mesh mono canvas, length depending on width of luggage rack, width 5″. Paternayan wool yarn. Luggage rack from Sudbury House.

COLORS: Background—260 or 261 White
Triangles—662 and 661 Pine Green
950 and 952 Strawberry
511 and 512 Old Blue
727 Autumn Yellow

STITCHES: Basketweave. Work with 2-ply.

DIRECTIONS: Work each strip from upper right hand corner down following graph. Colors of triangles are random.

NOTES: See sections on *STITCHES, ADDITIONAL PROJECTS*.

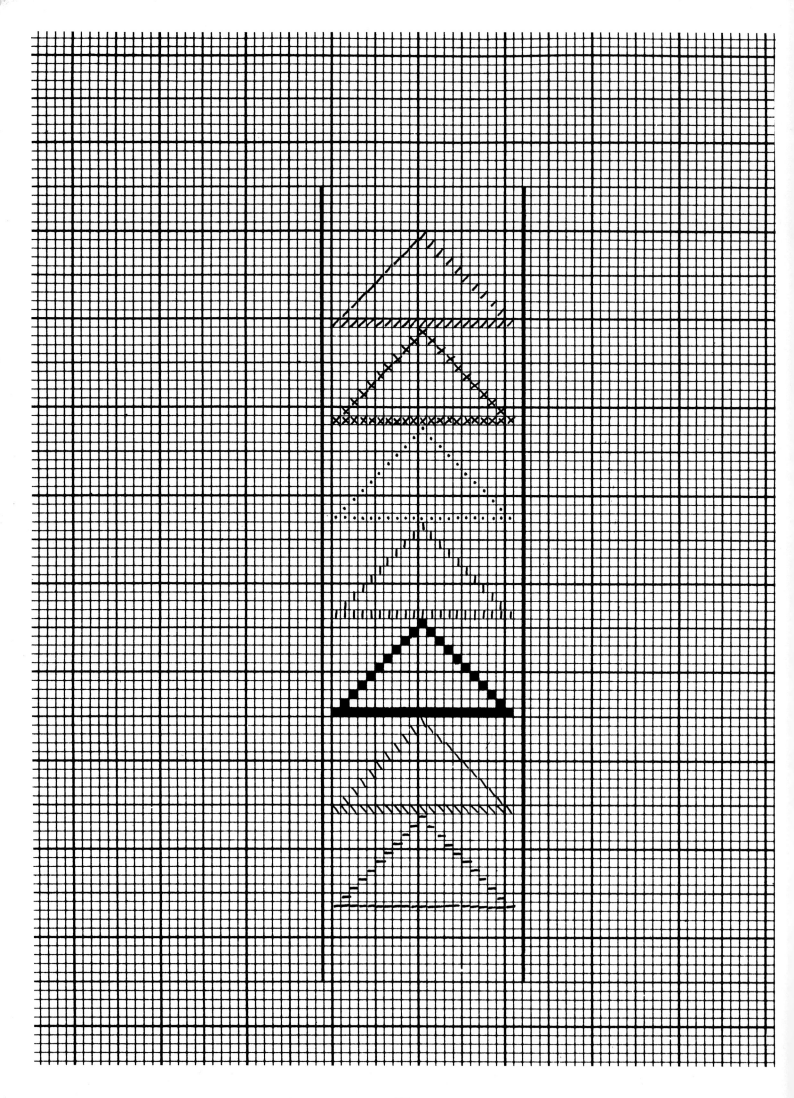

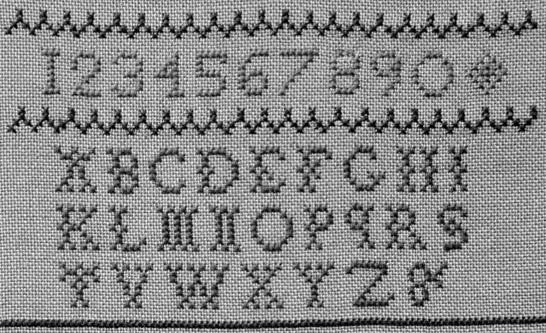

Sampler

A short version of a wonderful Balch School sampler wrought in the 18th century, from Providence, Rhode Island. This version is quick to stitch and gives the elements of a truly old and lovely piece of work.

MATERIALS: Natural linen, 28 count, DMC cotton floss.

COLORS: Red (letters) 3328, Yellow (windows and walk) 3078, Light Green (grass) 320, Dark Green (trees) 936, Light Beige (roof and windows) 842, Medium Grey (fence) 645, Dark Brown (tree trunks and walk) 3021, Dark Grey (borders) 844, Light Blue (house) 794, Dark Blue (numbers) 931.

STITCHES: Counted Cross-Stitch. 2 strands DMC over two threads.

DIRECTIONS: Mark center of fabric. Count up and over to top border and begin. Work in rows, working down. Press. Frame.

NOTES: See sections on *COUNTED CROSS-STITCH, BLOCKING, ADDITIONAL PROJECTS.*

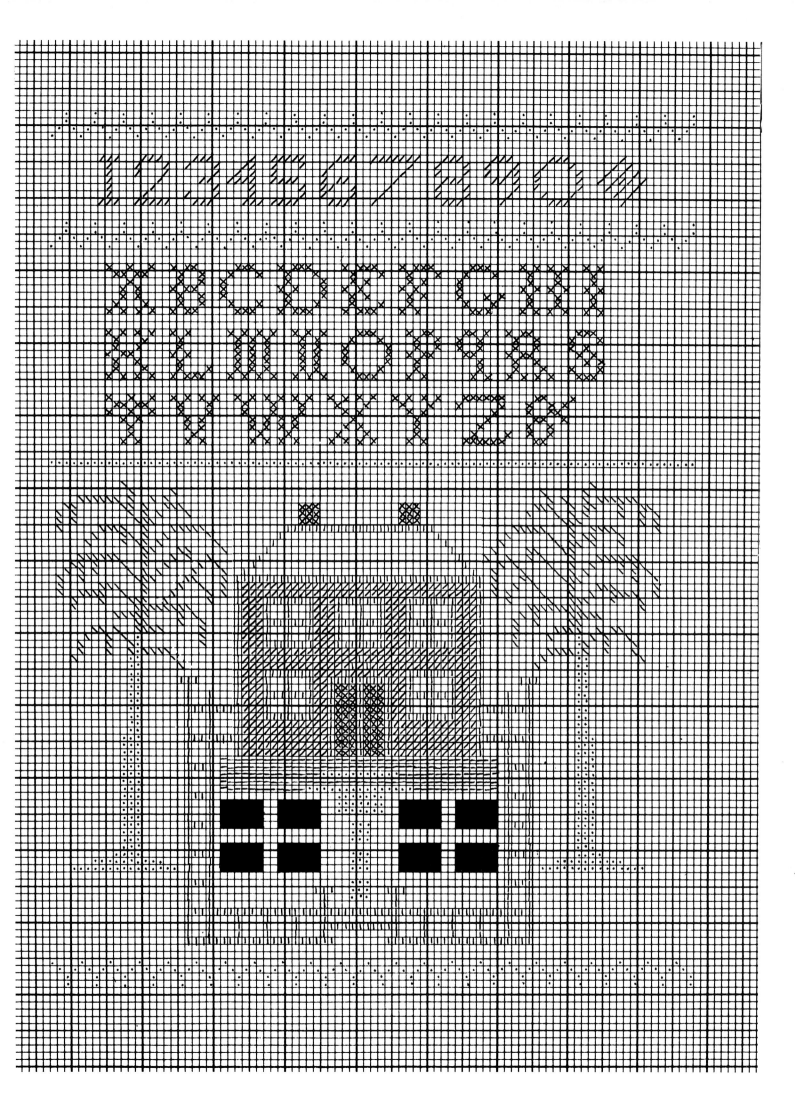

Patchwork Star Tote Bag

A perky little tote, this interesting pattern is adapted from a 19th-century quilt. It works up nicely into a tote bag insert. Expanded and worked as a pillow would be smashing. Lots of potential for this pattern.

MATERIALS: Tote bag, from Cottage Needlepoint, 13 mesh mono canvas, DMC Pearl cotton floss.

COLORS:
746 Off-White
991 Dark Aquamarine
598 Light Turquoise
930 Dark Antique Blue
518 Light Wedgewood
932 Light Antique Blue
890 Ultra-Dark Pistachio Green
444 Dark Lemon
744 Pale Yellow
352 Light Coral
776 Medium Pink
951 Flesh
353 Peach Flesh
402 Light Mahogany

STITCHES: Continental, Mosaic, Smyrna Cross.

DIRECTIONS: Find center of canvas. Work out from center in blocks following graph and colors as marked. Bind edges after trimming and insert into tote.

NOTES: See sections on *NEEDLEPOINT NOTES, BLOCKING, ADDITIONAL PROJECTS.*

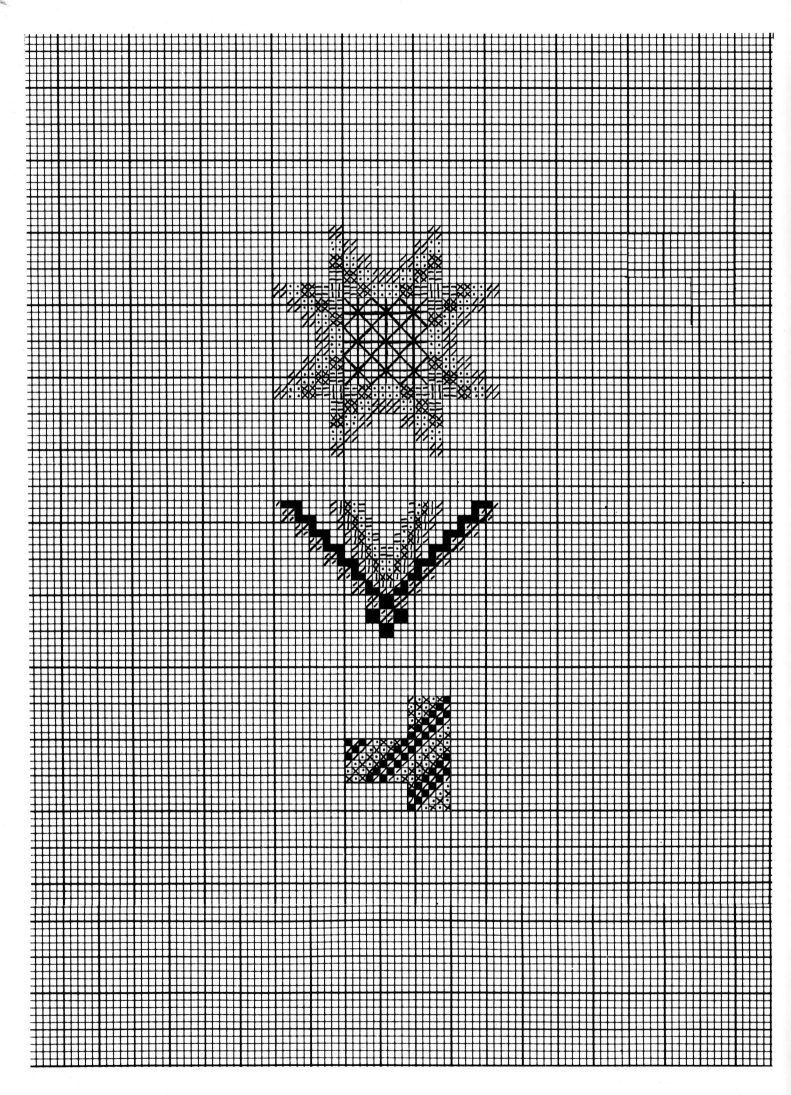

Watermelon Bordered Hand Towels

Want a very personal and quick gift idea? Try making sets of these decorative little hand towels. They are quick and easy, charming and useful. Try other motifs from this book in place of watermelons for lots of variety.

MATERIALS: 14 count tan border towels, DMC cotton floss.

COLORS: 936—Dark Green
               3012—Light Green
               746—Cream
               347—Red
               310—Black

STITCHES: Counted Cross-Stitch. Work with 6 strands.

DIRECTIONS: Find center of border and center of graph. Work in either direction.

NOTES: See sections on *COUNTED CROSS-STITCH, ADDITIONAL PROJECTS.*

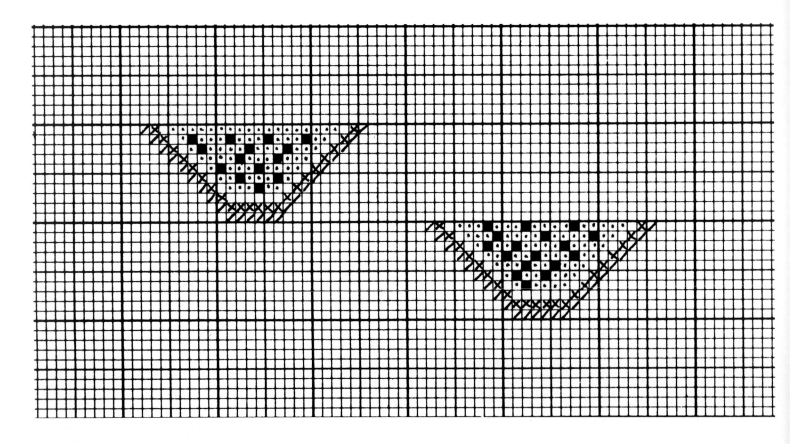

Country Goose Pillow

The ever-popular goose makes an appearance here on a checked bordered pillow. A whimsical butterfly dances about while a fence sets off the background.

MATERIALS: 13 mesh mono canvas, 16″ x 16″. Paternayan wool yarn

COLORS:
Border—500 Navy, 502 and 504 Federal Blue, 262 Off-white
Goose—262 Off-white
Fence—430 Dark Brown
Tulips—951 Strawberry
Tulip leaves—663 Pine Green
Grass—661 Pine Green
Sky—504 Federal Blue
Goose beak—727 Autumn Yellow

FINISHED SIZE: 12″ x 12″

STITCHES: Basketweave and backstitch. Work with 2-ply.

DIRECTIONS: Find center of canvas. Count out and work Goose. Work fence, sky, grass and tulips. Work border.

NOTES: See sections on *NEEDLEPOINT NOTES, STITCHES, BLOCKING, ADDITIONAL PROJECTS.*

Indian Blanket Sport Tote Bag

For the "sporty" man in your life, here is a wonderful sport tote complete with tennis pocket. A needlepoint window at the end allows you to personalize this tote. We've used a portion of the Indian Blanket pattern which makes a very handsome combination.

MATERIALS: Sport Tote, from Cottage Needlepoint, 10 mesh mono canvas, S&C Huber 2-ply wool yarn or Paternayan wool yarn, darning needle.

COLORS: S&C Huber yarn can be ordered directly from S&C Huber. Ask for Indian Blanket yarn.
Paternayan—830 Bittersweet
311 Grape
472 Toast Brown
464 Beige Brown
542 Cobalt Blue
421 Chocolate Brown

STITCHES: Continental. Work with 2-ply Huber yarn or 3-ply Paternayan.

DIRECTIONS: Find center of canvas and count up to beginning of graph. Work according to graph changing colors randomly for varigated look. Bind edges after trimming and insert into tote.

NOTES: See sections on *NEEDLEPOINT NOTES, BLOCKING, ADDITIONAL PROJECTS.*

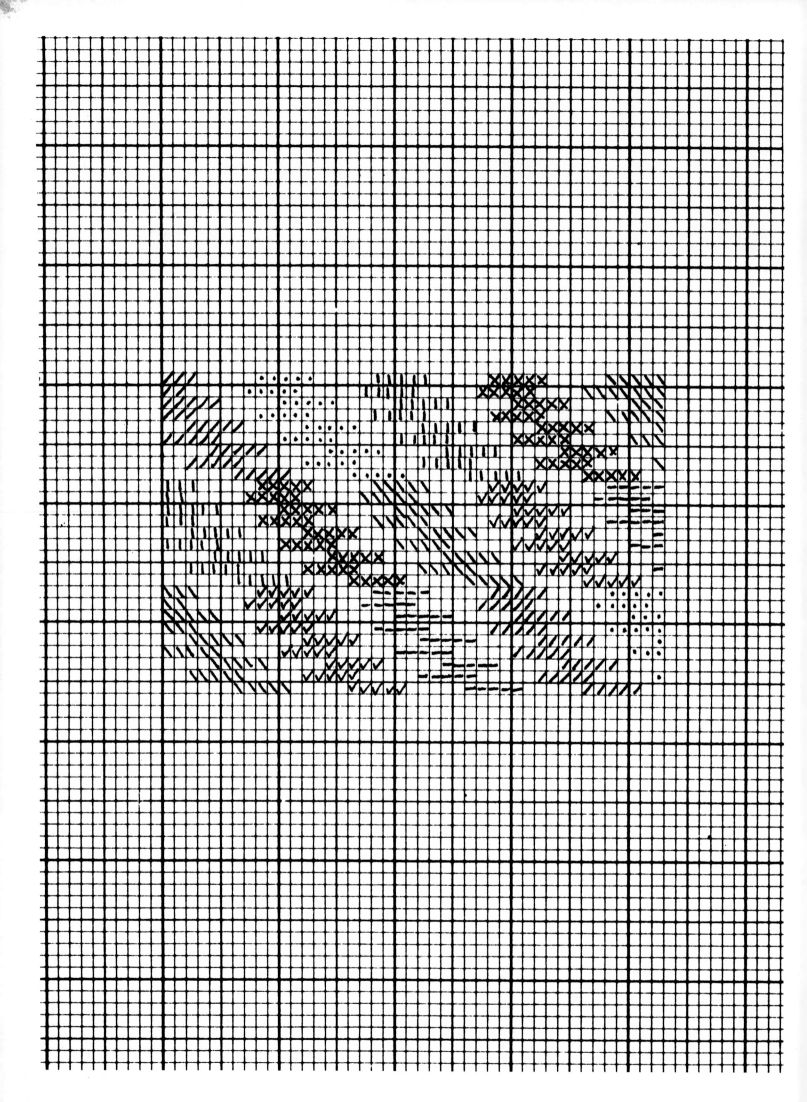

46

Indian Blanket Belt

This wonderful belt is another Indian-inspired design. Its muted colors and tweedy look help it combine nicely with a casual wardrobe. Colors can be used at random or planned as a repeat pattern. Either way it looks great!

MATERIALS: 10 mesh mono canvas, length of belt plus 4 inches and 5 inch width, S&C Huber Indian Blanket yarn or Paternayan wool yarn, darning needle.

COLORS: S&C Huber yarn can be ordered directly from S&C Huber. Ask for Indian Blanket yarn.

Paternayan—830 Bittersweet
311 Grape
472 Toast Brown
464 Beige Brown
542 Cobalt Blue
421 Chocolate Brown

STITCHES: Continental. Work with 2-ply Huber yarn or 3-ply Paternayan.

DIRECTIONS: Find center of canvas and work from middle toward ends. Needlepoint on belt will be 1¼ inches plus 2 extra rows of background needlepoint along each edge. (These rows will be folded under when belt is mounted.)

NOTES: See sections on *NEEDLEPOINT NOTES, STITCHES, BELTS, BLOCKING, ADDITIONAL PROJECTS.*

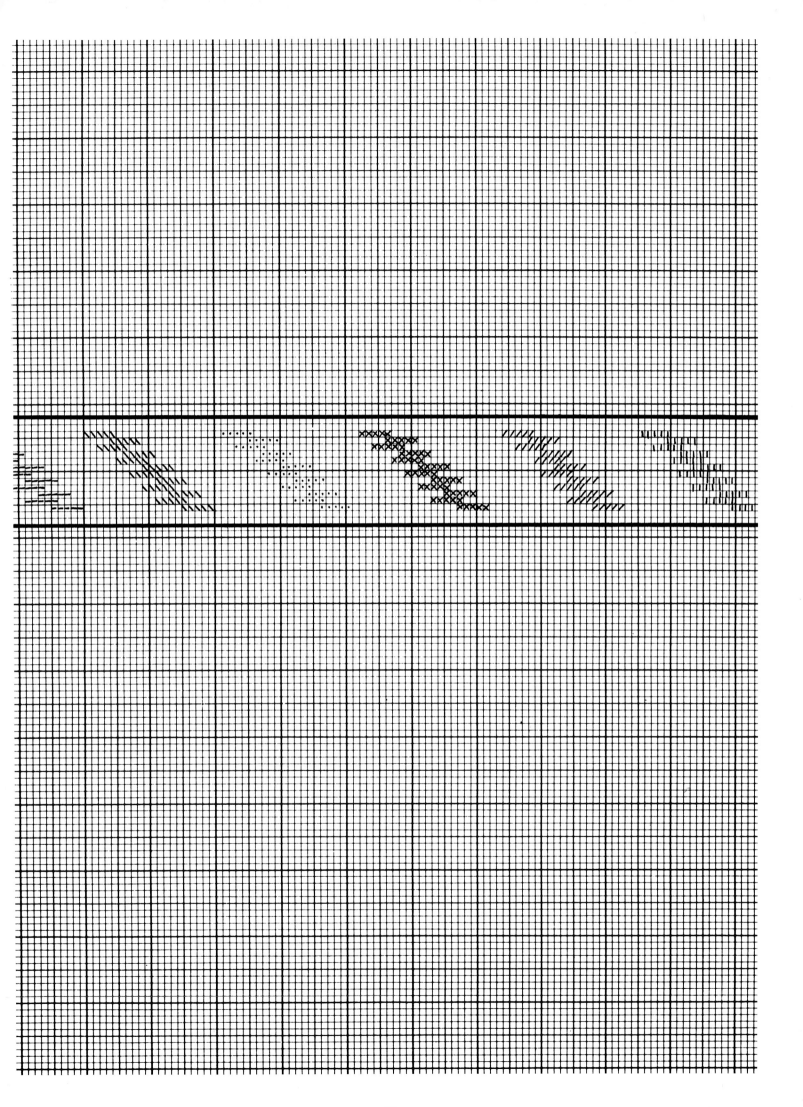

Indian Blanket Tote Bag

This smart-looking tote contains another variation of the Indian Blanket motif in a larger window than the Sport Tote. A great-looking tote, it will come in handy for men or women wherever they go.

MATERIALS: Large Tote, from Cottage Needlepoint, 10 mesh mono canvas, S&C Huber 2-ply wool yarn or Paternayan wool yarn, darning needle.

COLORS: S&C Huber yarn can be ordered directly from S&C Huber. Ask for Indian Blanket yarn.
Paternayan—830 Bittersweet
311 Grape
472 Toast Brown
464 Beige Brown
542 Cobalt Blue
421 Chocolate Brown

STITCHES: Continental or Basketweave. Work with 2-ply Huber yarn or 3-ply Paternayan.

DIRECTIONS: Find center of canvas and count up to beginning of graph. Work center portion and then sides. Bind edges after trimming and insert into tote.

NOTES: See sections on *NEEDLEPOINT NOTES, BLOCKING, ADDITIONAL PROJECTS.*

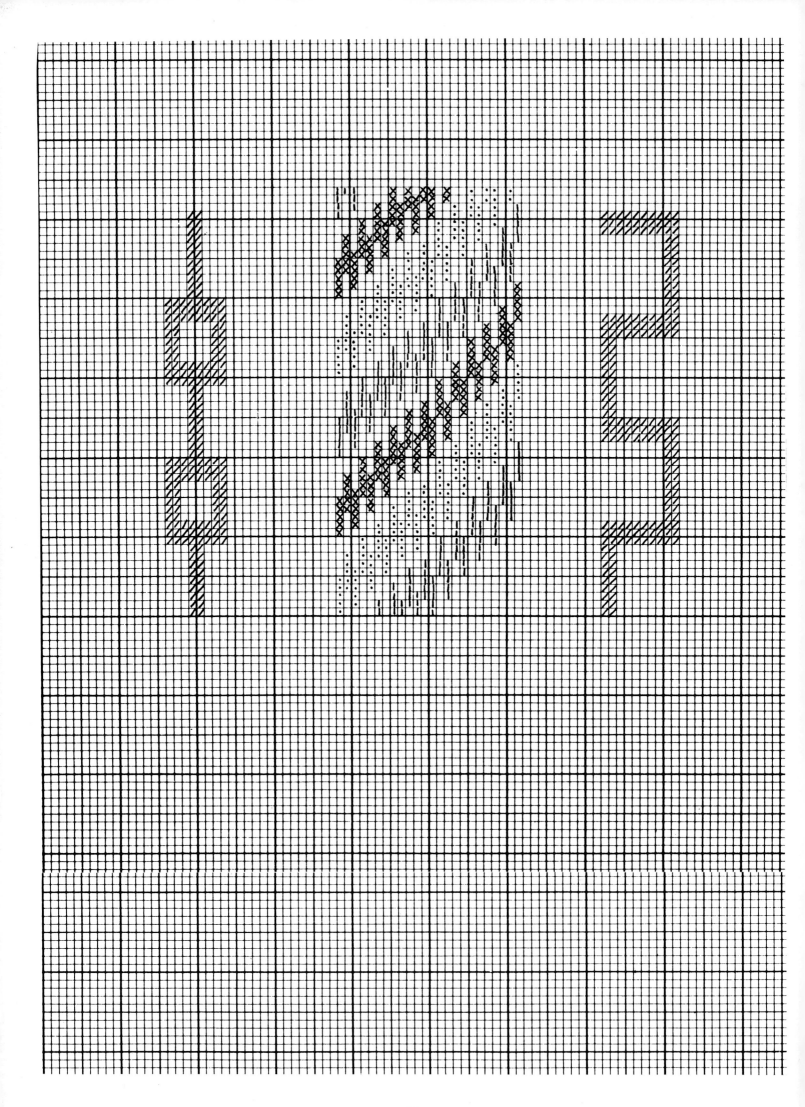

Indian Blanket Eyeglass Case

Another accessory from the Indian Blanket series is this good-looking eyeglass case. Suitable for men or women, it has a handsome textured finish. Try a check book cover to complete the set.

MATERIALS: 10 mesh mono canvas, to fit glasses plus 1″ on each side, S&C Huber 2-ply wool yarn or Paternayan wool yarn, darning needle, lining.

COLORS: S&C Huber yarn can be ordered directly from S&C Huber. Ask for Indian Blanket yarn.

Paternayan—830 Bittersweet
311 Grape
472 Toast Brown
464 Beige Brown
542 Cobalt Blue
421 Chocolate Brown

STITCHES: Continental. Work with 2-ply Huber yarn or 3-ply Paternayan.

DIRECTIONS: Find center of canvas and center of graph and work up and down following chart and using colors at random or in a planning design. Line and sew to desired size.

NOTES: See sections on *NEEDLEPOINT NOTES, STITCHES, BLOCKING, ADDITIONAL PROJECTS.*

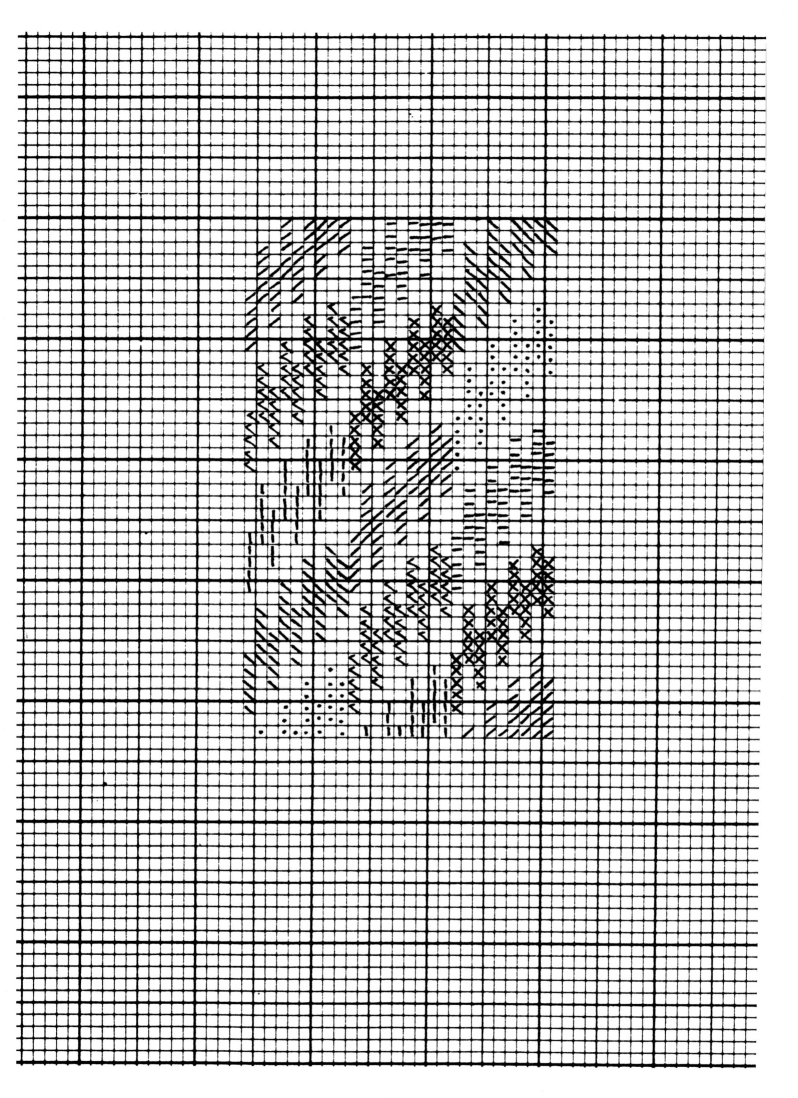

Shaker Tree-Of-Life Mirror

This famous Shaker Tree was painted by Sister Hannah Cohoon in 1854. Since that time it has graced many objects and been shown in a great variety of books, magazines and calendars. It looks particularly effective in this mirror, but will look wonderful no matter how you work it.

MATERIALS: Natural linen, 28 count, 8″ x 10″, DMC cotton floss, Sudbury House mirror.

COLORS: DMC 3328-Strawberry Red

STITCHES: Counted Cross-Stitch. Work with 2 strands over 2 threads.

DIRECTIONS: Find center of fabric and center of chart and work from center out. Press. Insert into frame.

NOTES: See sections on *COUNTED CROSS-STITCH, BLOCKING, ADDITIONAL PROJECTS.*

Moored Boats Tray

This "yachty"-looking tray is perfect for the sailors in your life. Moored boats are silhouetted against a solid background. This pattern is striking in the reverse combination also.

MATERIALS: Navy Aida fabric—14 count, 15″ x 15″, DMC embroidery floss, Sudbury House tray.

COLORS: DMC—Blanc Neige-White

STITCHES: Counted Cross-Stitch. Work with 2 strands.

DIRECTIONS: Find center of fabric. Work center boats in cross-stitch, work others from inside moving outward. From alphabet chart work desired name at bottom.

NOTES: See sections on *CROSS-STITCH, BLOCKING, ADDITIONAL PROJECTS.*

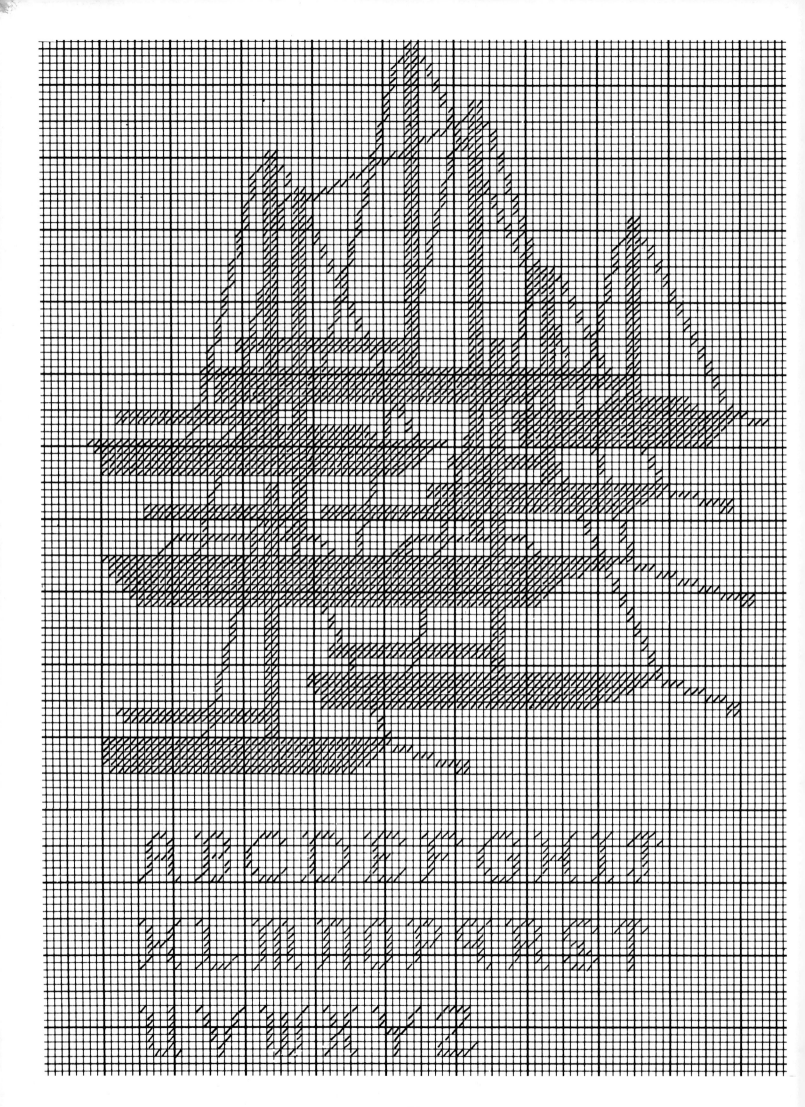

Indiana Fan
Crew-Neck Pullover

Indiana Fan Tote Bag

A wild and crazy 19th-century quilt pattern, the Indiana Fan is sometimes referred to as Drunkard's Path. It's colorful, fun, and very Pop-art looking. We think you will find it great for a multitude of projects.

MATERIALS: Tote bag with opening for needlepoint, from Cottage Needlepoint, 13 mesh mono canvas to fit tote plus 1″ on each side, Paternayan wool yarn.

COLORS: Background colors—220 Black, 221 Charcoal, 201 Steel Gray.

Fans—741 Tobacco, 502 Federal Blue, 498 Flesh, 523 Teal Blue, 714 Mustard, 755 Old Gold, 954 Strawberry, 603 Forest Green, 860 Copper, 862 Copper, 500 Federal Blue, 952 Strawberry, 727 Autumn Yellow, and 660 Pine Green.

STITCHES: Continental or Basketweave. Work with 2-ply.

DIRECTIONS: Cut canvas to fit opening for tote plus 1″ on each side. Find center of canvas and work from center out following graph. Bind edges after trimming and insert into tote.

NOTES: See sections on *NEEDLEPOINT NOTES, BLOCKING, ADDITIONAL PROJECTS.*

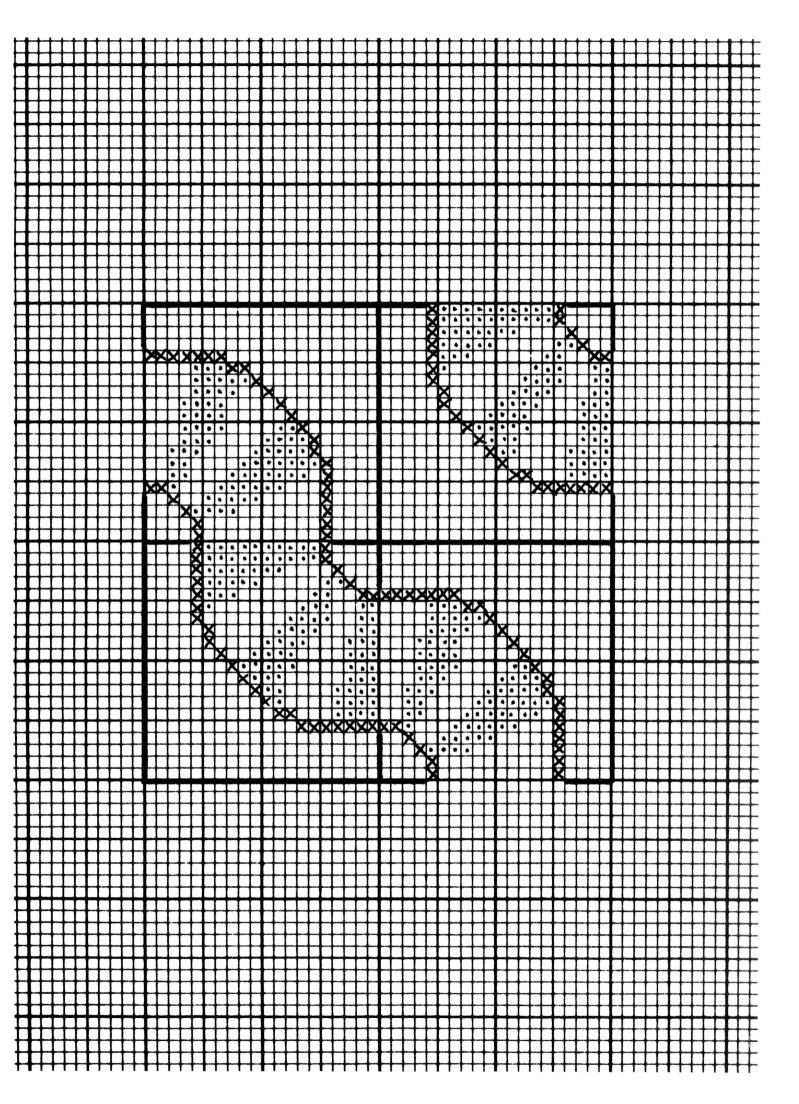

Towne Border—Case, Cover, and Bag

An 18th-century Towne Border works up nicely into an eyeglass case, a check book cover, and a cosmetic bag. This architectural design, inspired by a Jacquard coverlet, combines a variety of houses, trees and fencing. Easily adapted for many other uses.

MATERIALS: Delft Blue Aida fabric—14 count, 15″ x 18″, DMC embroidery floss, coordinated fabric for lining, zipper for cosmetic bag, black bias corded piping.

COLORS: DMC 310 Black

STITCHES: Counted Cross-Stitch. Work with 2 strands.

DIRECTIONS: Cut Aida cloth into three pieces measuring: 7½″ x 18″, and two 7½″ x 9″ (the cosmetic bag is the larger of the three pieces). With ½″ seam allowance on all sides, work the border pattern. Add lining, zipper and piping as required, leaving slots for check book.

NOTES: See sections on *CROSS-STITCH, BLOCKING, ADDITIONAL PROJECTS.*

Oriental Rug Boxes

The patterns on these handsome wooden boxes are derived from an antique Oriental rug. The dark rich colors blend nicely with wood tones and the patterns can easily be adapted for other projects.

MATERIALS: 13 mesh mono canvas, size to fit box plus 1 inch on all sides, Paternayan wool yarn, wooden boxes from Sudbury House, cardboard, stuffing, navy braid.

COLORS: Large box—862 Copper, Background
                    500 Federal Blue, Diamonds
                    860 Copper, Triangles on border and middle of central motif
                    741 Tobacco, Outside stripe on central motif

              Small box—862 Copper, Background
                    860 Copper, Center motif and middle band
                    741 Tobacco, Outside band
                    498 Hazelnut Brown, Center of diamond
                    500 Federal Blue, Blue lines

STITCHES: Continental. Work with 2-ply.

DIRECTIONS: Find center of canvas and graph. Work central emblem and continue out to central diamond. Work diamond pattern on sides. Fill in background. Back with medium weight fabric and cardboard, stuff slightly. Attach braid and insert into box.

NOTES: See sections on *NEEDLEPOINT NOTES, BLOCKING, ADDITIONAL PROJECTS.*

73

Reindeer and Pine Trees Tray

A take-off on the "classic" reindeer. These folky reindeer are adapted from a 19th-century hooked rug. They are a great addition to the Holiday Season. Shown here in traditional reds and greens, this pattern can be used for a whole array of other projects.

MATERIALS: Red Aida fabric with a 14 count, 15″ x 12″ (or size to fit tray). Tray—Petite Serving tray by Sudbury House. DMC embroidery floss, Balger Blending Filament, Offray ribbon ⅝″, 1½ yards.

COLORS: Reindeer—3046 Honey gold, 3 strands

Trees—895 pine green, 3 strands plus 1 Balger Blending Filament—Peacock

Eyes—310 black, 2 strands plus 1 Balger Blending Filament—Peacock

STITCHES: Counted Cross-Stitch.

DIRECTIONS: Find center of fabric and work center tree. Work reindeer and other trees. Place ribbon in place and tack down. Staple or tack to edge of tray.

NOTES: See sections on *CROSS-STITCH, BLOCKING, ADDITIONAL PROJECTS*.

Flower and Vine Footstool

A warm and inviting country pattern, this flower and grid design looks great in any color combination. Paired with pillows, this footstool makes a great accent for any room or armchair.

MATERIALS: 13 mesh mono canvas, size of bench plus 5 inches on each side, Paternayan wool yarn. Footstool from Sudbury House.

COLORS: Background—462 Beige Brown
Flowers—951 Strawberry, 521 Teal Blue, 727 Autumn Yellow, 922 Wood Rose.
Vines—660 Pine Green

STITCHES: Basketweave for background. Continental for flowers. Work with 2-ply.

DIRECTIONS: Find center of canvas and work center flower. Work vines in all four directions. Work remainder of flowers. Fill in background.

NOTES: See sections on *STITCHES, ADDITIONAL PROJECTS.*

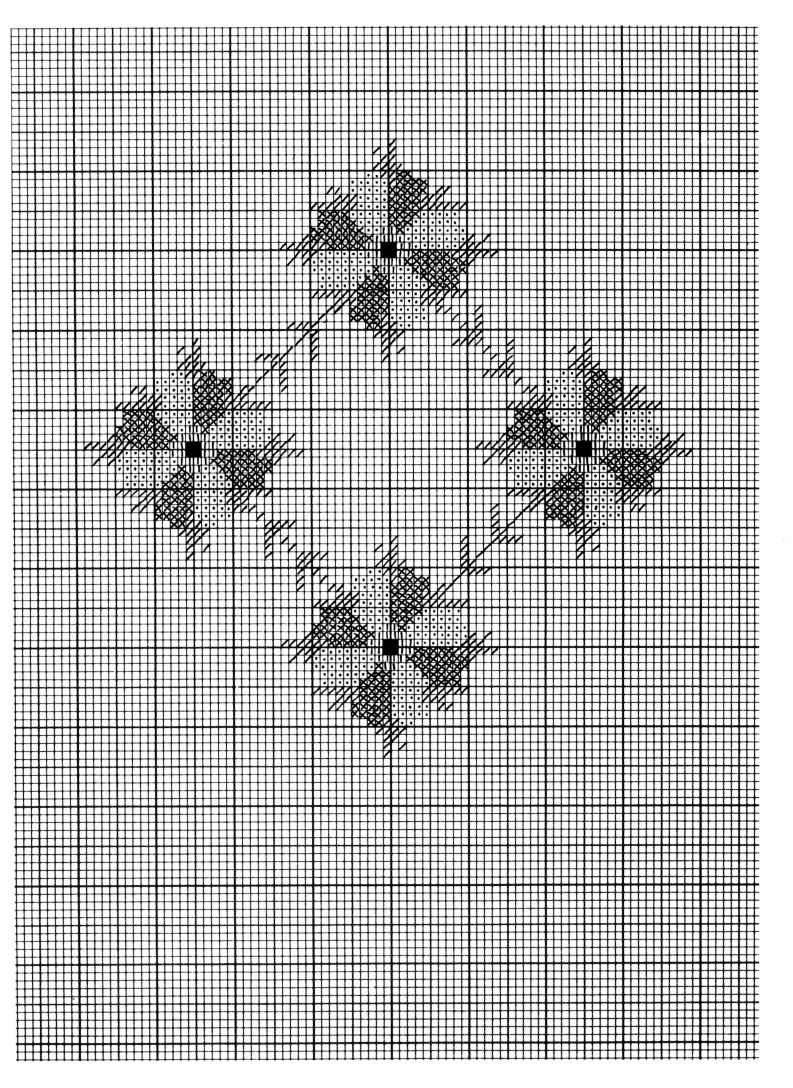

Irish Chain Carriage House Clock

The ever-popular Irish Chain, in this case Triple Irish Chain, has been a classic since the 19th century. Here it simply tells the time.

MATERIALS: Soft pink linen, 28 count, 6″ x 8″ piece, DMC cotton floss, Sudbury House Carriage Clock.

COLORS: DMC 3078 Yellow, 794 Blue, 504 Green

STITCHES: Counted Cross-Stitch. Work with 2 strands.

DIRECTIONS: Find center of fabric. Count up to top and work graph from top to bottom. Press. Insert in clock as per directions with clock.

NOTES: See sections on *COUNTED CROSS-STITCH, BLOCKING, ADDITIONAL PROJECTS.*

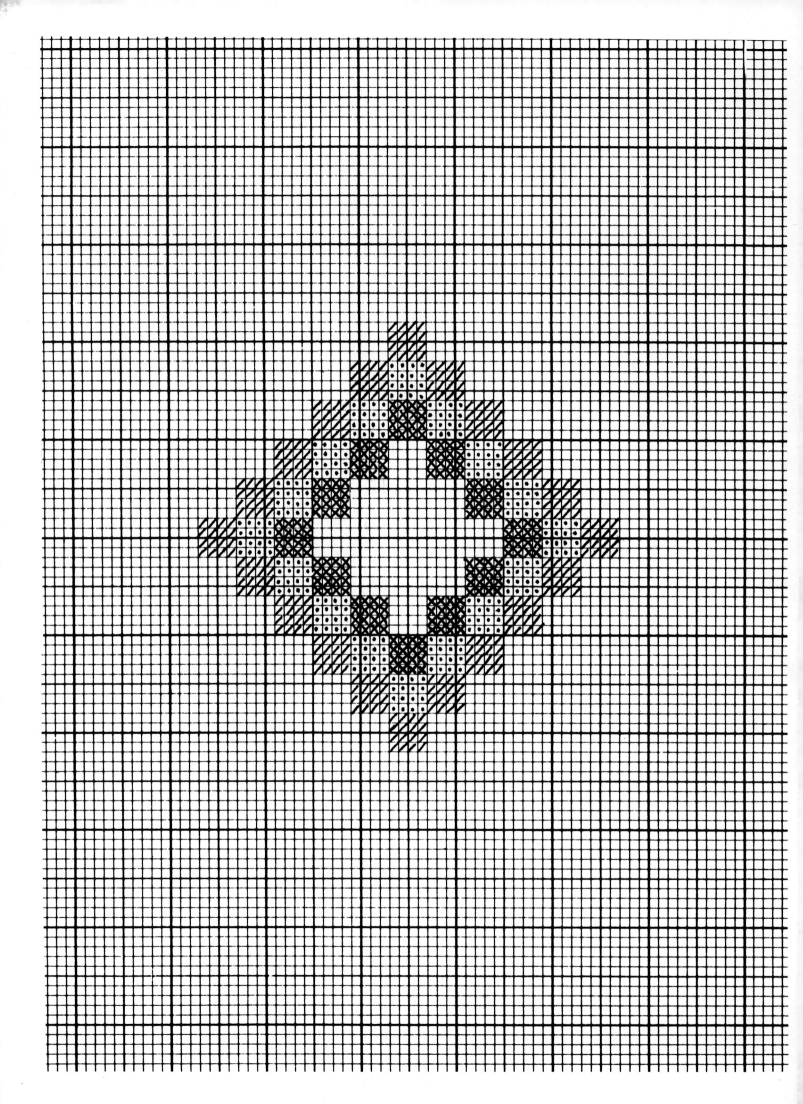

Checked Table Runner With House Border

A center chimney house and flowers decorate the ends of this checked table runner, or towel. A quick and easy project with a personal touch, it's a nice accessory for any decor.

MATERIALS: 11 count towelling, DMC cotton floss.

COLORS:

Roof—939 Dark Blue
House—3328 Strawberry Red
Door and Chimney—3012 (back stitch)
Door—794 Blue
Windows—3078 Yellow
Flowers—321 Red
Stems and Leaves—936

STITCHES: Counted Cross-Stitch, Back Stitch. Work with 6 strands.

DIRECTIONS: Find center of border. Find center of house on graph and work outwards. Count over and work flowers.

NOTES: See sections on *COUNTED CROSS-STITCH, ADDITIONAL PROJECTS.*

Wooden plates available from S & C Huber

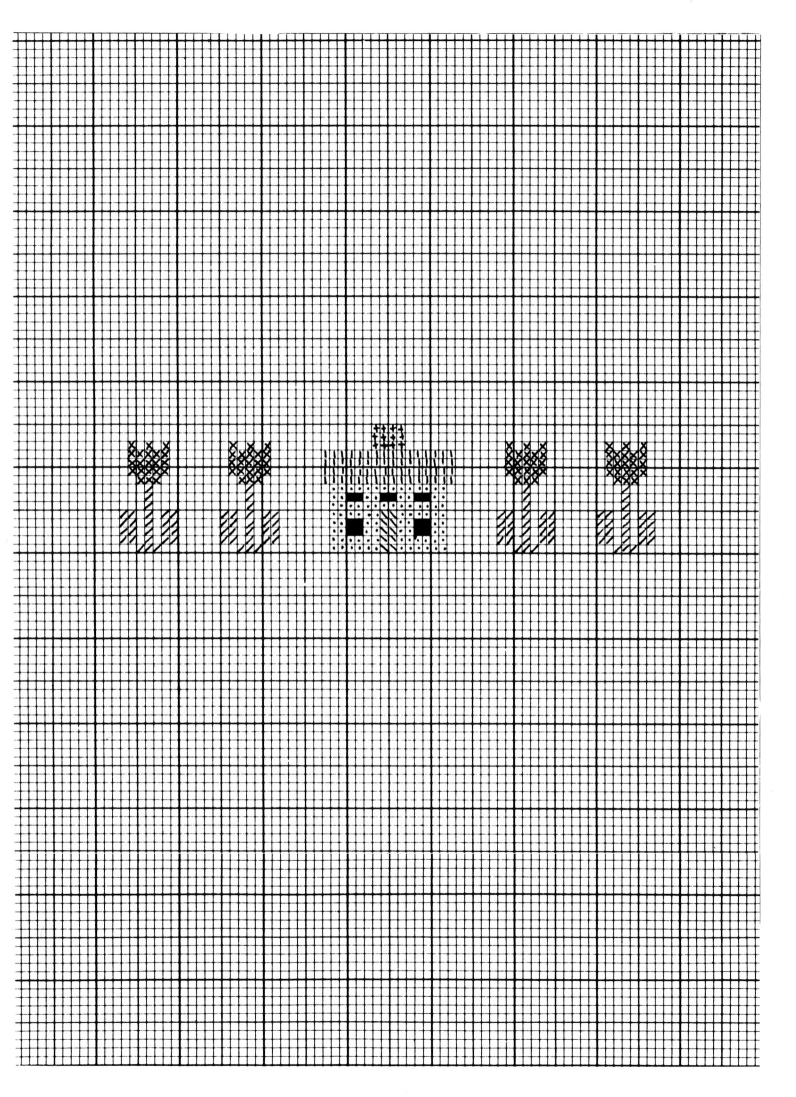

Smutt-The-Cat Pillow

Smutt, the most famous of all folk-art cats, is seen here gracing a wonderful pillow. Painted in the 19th century, he is found in numerous books and calendars. The variety of stitches combine to make a beautiful and textured pillow.

MATERIALS: 16″ x 16″, 13 mesh mono canvas, #18 or 20 tapestry needle, Paternayan wool yarn for Smutt, rug and background, DMC embroidery floss for rug and whiskers.

COLORS: Smutt's stripes: Gold—tweed one strand of each color together to make a new color 727 and 714. Rust—860 and 862.

Chest—tweed one strand of each color together to make a new color, 262 and 755.

Smutt's chin—498

Smutt's whiskers—Any color beige to rust embroidery floss.

Rug—tweed one strand of each color together to make a new color, 523 and 603 Paternayan and 3023 DMC embroidery floss.

Flowers—tweed one strand of each color together to make a new color 951 and 953, 952 and 954, makes light and dark color of flowers.

Center of Flowers—922

Leaves—660

Background—600

FINISHED SIZE   12″ x 12″ pillow.

STITCHES: Smutt's chest—Upside-down Kalem. Background—Long-armed Cross or Greek Stitch (Stavropounti). Rest of chart done in Continental. Work with 2-ply.

DIRECTIONS: Find center of canvas to start (see Needlepoint Notes). Count out to the outline of Smutt and work outline. Outline rug. Fill in cat, rug and flowers. Work background. Lay down whiskers when completely finished. Come up at mouth area and stitch to length of whisker. One long thread. Couching should not be necessary.

NOTES: See sections on *STITCHES, TWEEDING, ADDITIONAL PROJECTS.*

Heart and Hand Candlewick Pillow

A lacy pillow with a Victorian flair, this special design is carried over from a long-ago romantic period. Worked here in Candlewicking technique, it can be transposed to Needlepoint or Counted Cross-Stitch. We have worked up two designs, one for a large pillow, the other for a small pillow. Directions are given for the larger size.

MATERIALS: 5 pieces of muslin 18″ square, Lily or J&P Coats Candlewick yarn, 6 inch x 4 yards muslin, 4 yards of 2½ inch cotton lace, 2 pieces of 18″ quilt batting, polyfill.

STITCHES: French Knots, Backstitch. Work with 2 strands Candlewick yarn.

DIRECTIONS: Find center of fabric. Trace pattern from book onto tracing paper. Mark on fabric with fabric marking pen or fabric carbon. (Make sure marks will come off.) Stitch as per graph, working hands in backstitch, hearts with three rows of colonial knots close together and remainder with 1 row of colonial knots ¼″ apart. To finish: Cut 4 extra 18″ squares of muslin and 2–18″ squares of quilt batting. Make "sandwich" with batting in middle, pin and stitch around and treat as single piece. Cut 6″ pieces of muslin crosswise to 4 yard dimension. Sew strips together and sew 2 short ends together, being careful not to twist. Fold in half lengthwise and press. Make French seam in short ends of lace. Lay on top of ruffle and stitch together. Now you can treat ruffle pieces as one. Quarter ruffle and gather. Pin to pillow front matching quarter markers with corners. Sew. Lay second "sandwich" on top. Pin and sew around three sides and all four corners, leaving bottom open for stuffing. Turn pillow inside out, remove pins and make sure ruffle has not been caught. Turn back outside in and clip corners. Turn back, stuff and stitch opening closed.

NOTES: See sections on *CANDLEWICK, ADDITIONAL PROJECTS*.

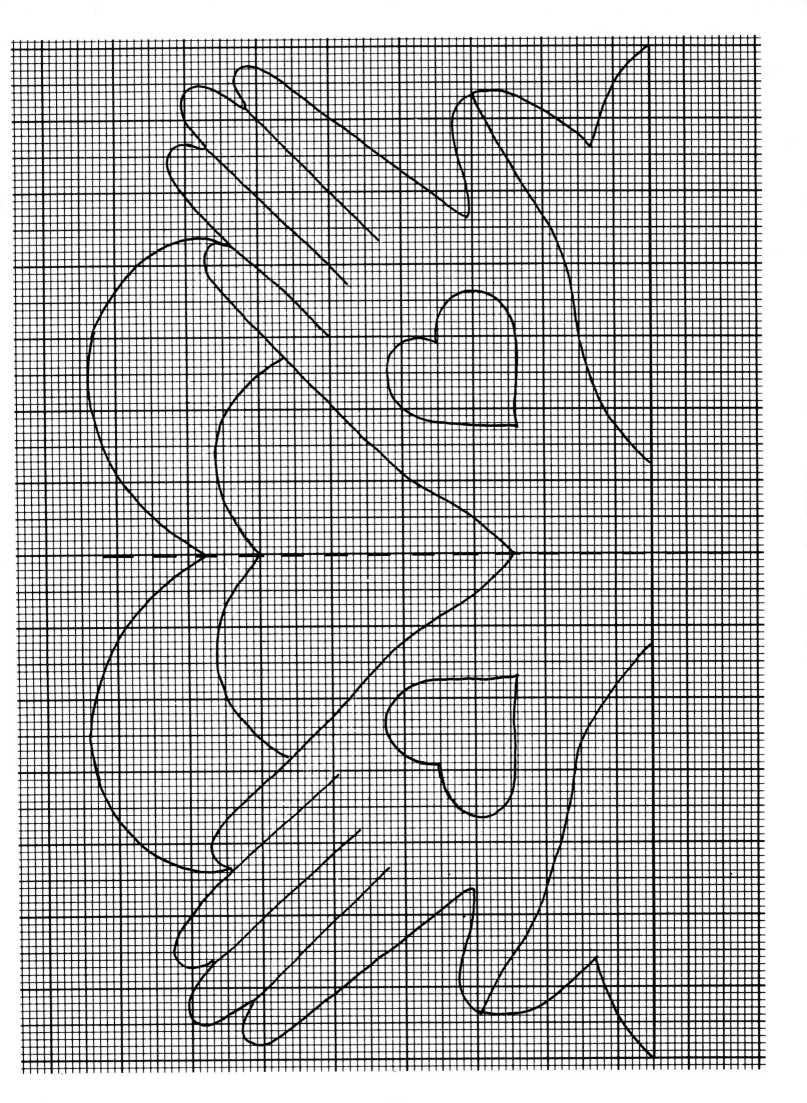

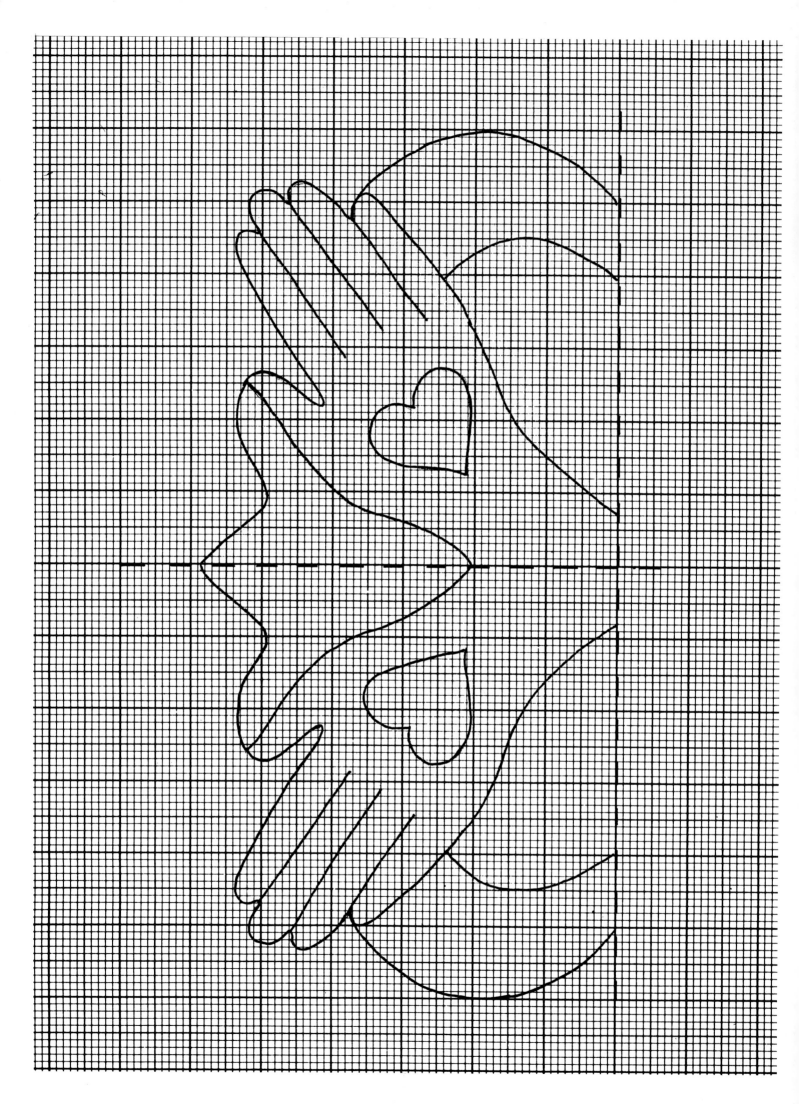

SUPPLIERS

American Crewel & Canvas Studio
Route 2, Box 224B
Parsonsburg, MD 21849

Yarns, canvas and fabric.

A. Zeller Belt Mfg. Co.
3269 Walter Avenue
St. Louis, MO 63143

Belts and belt finishing.
Wholesale ONLY, no retail.

Best Friends Finishing (Martha Neal)
75 Polland Road
Mountain Lakes, NJ 07046

Professional finishing
for all types of needlework.

Cottage Needlepoint
8198 Mink Road, Box 313
Harbor Springs, MI 49740

Tote bags and other supplies.

Exemplarery
P.O. Box 2554-H
Dearborn, MI 48123

18th-century reproduction sampler kits.
Catalog $2.50

Freeman & Co.
416 Julian Avenue
Thomasville, NC 27360

Furniture for needlework.

Heart of the Needle (Jacqui Clarkson)
38 West Main Street
Rockaway, NJ 07866

Cross-stitch and needleworks supplies.

Johnson Creative Crafts
445 Main Street
West Townsend, MA 01474

Yarns, canvas, fabric and much more.

K's Creations
P.O. Box 161446
Austin, TX 78746

Frames for needlework.

Needlepoint Country (Betty Voulgaris)
104 Mine Brook Road
Bernardsville, NJ 07924

Belt finishing and needlepoint supplies,
painted canvases.

S & C Huber, American Classics
82 Plants Dam Road
East Lyme, CT 06333

Yarn for Indian blanket, $6.00 for eyeglass,
belt, or sport tote. $8.00 for large tote,
pp. knitting books and kits. Catalog $2.50

Sudbury House
Colton Road, Box 895
Old Lyme, CT 06371

Furniture, boxes, trays, coasters, clocks and
much more.

Notes

Notes

Notes